Social Media for Home-Based Businesses

Table of Contents

Your culture is your brand.

— Tony Hsieh

Chapter 1. Introduction

Has the digital age opened up fresh, exciting opportunities for you? Are you trying to leverage social media platforms to grow your home-based business massively but feeling overwhelmed about where to start? Then, you'll certainly want to reach out for this invigorating Special Report on "Social Media for Home-Based Businesses". This easy to comprehend, cheerfully written dossier takes you through the fascinating world of social media, offering strategic insights, useful tips, and clear-cut, practical guidance. It is kindled not just to educate but also inspire you to unlock a world of unlimited potential to grow your home-based business. Just by reading this report, you'll be armed with actionable steps that are sure to propel your business to dizzying heights. So are you ready to ride the wave of social media success?

Chapter 2. Understanding Social Media Landscape: An Overview

Social media, as we know intimately and unequivocally, has revolutionized the tenor and texture of human interactions, its breachless walls bundling together the dispersed global community into a bustling neighborhood. In the world of business, especially those nestled snugly at homes, it has expanded and transformed the market landscape, opening up a repertoire of striking possibilities. This chapter transports you on an enlightening journey across this expansive social media landscape.

2.1. The Evolution of Social Media

Right from the basic bulletin board systems and chat rooms of the early internet era to today's cornucopia of innovative platforms, social media's journey mirrors and encapsulates the breathtaking evolution of technology.

It started as a nascent form of interaction in the late 20th century when chat rooms like AOL enabled people across the globe to connect and engage. Entering the 21st century, the advent of Friendster and MySpace elevated this concept, offering people spaces to share their life through digital narratives. These platforms nudged their way into becoming potent catalysts of social change, instigating a new form of global solidarity.

The birth of Facebook and Twitter in the mid-2000s marked a seismic shift in the social media landscape. Facebook offered a unified platform for communication, sharing images, videos, and instant messaging. Twitter introduced an innovative concept of 'microblogging', enabling users to share brief updates, news, and other content, effectively saturating a constantly thirsty news cycle.

This was just the beginning of a headlong flood that luged several other platforms into the mix. Instagram's focus shifted to visual content, LinkedIn tightened its grip on the professional realm, Snapchat flavoured it with ephemeral photo stories, while YouTube and TikTok captured the video content market.

This evolution persists unabated, with newer platforms and novel features being added perpetually, each moulding the landscape to create niche communities and to suit shifting user preferences.

2.2. Understanding the Major Social Media Platforms

To grasp the full potential of social media, it's crucial to gain an understanding of the currently leading platforms. Each platform is a unique ecosystem teeming with different demographics, behavioral trends, and user habits.

Facebook: The colossus of social media platforms, Facebook boasts over two billion active users. Its vast user base spans different age groups, although a majority of its users fall between 18 and 34 years. Businesses can create specialized pages, run targeted ad campaigns, broadcast live videos, and create groups fostering in-depth interactions.

Twitter: Billed as the 'go-to' platform for real-time news and conversation, Twitter thrives on its simplicity and speed. With 330 million users, it's a fertile ground for businesses looking to create cultural commentaries, participate in trending discussions, launch customer service initiatives or simply share quick updates.

Instagram: A visually centric platform, Instagram has over a billion active users dominated by the younger demographic. From stunning product photographs to behind-the-scenes stories, businesses can use Instagram's myriad features to connect with followers on a visceral and aesthetic level.

LinkedIn: This professional networking platform hosts 774 million users. LinkedIn offers businesses a channel to build professional relationships, promote thought leadership, recruit talent and position themselves as industry experts.

YouTube: A video-sharing platform par excellence, YouTube holds an extensive user base across all age groups. Businesses can leverage it to create engaging video content, like product demos, tutorials, webinars and interviews, to reach a broader audience.

TikTok: TikTok boasts over 800 million active users skewed to a younger demographic, making it an excellent platform for businesses to adopt a fun, creative angle to engage with potential customers.

Other platforms like Pinterest, Snapchat, Reddit, provide brand unique appeal and distinct demographics for certain businesses to tap into.

2.3. The Impact of Social Media on Businesses

Social media has dramatically transformed businesses. It gives businesses the opportunity to engage and connect with customers at an unparalleled scale. It empowers home-based businesses to compete with larger competitors, enhances brand visibility, enables proactive customer service, and leverages the power of user-generated content for promotion.

Moreover, social media advertising allows businesses to target a specific demographic. This precision targeting not only improves the return on investment but also ensures that ads reach the relevant audience, a luxury traditional advertising channels do not offer.

Social media analytics is another important facet. Businesses can measure and analyze the performance of their posts through audience engagement parameters like likes, comments, shares, and more. Understanding these numbers powers strategic decisions, aiding businesses to tailor content in line with what resonates the most with their followers.

2.4. Challenges in the Social Media Space

Despite its numerous benefits, social media poses certain challenges. Ensuring consistent engagement, managing negative feedback, maintaining content quality, and keeping pace with the rapidly changing trends are just a few examples.

Mismanagement of social media profiles can lead to a tarnished brand image. Each post, comment, or tweet reflects on the business, thus it is essential to have a well-structured social media strategy and a crisis management plan.

Despite these challenges, the potential benefits far outweigh the risks, making it too invaluable an avenue for home-based businesses to ignore. With the right strategies, you can navigate these complexities and unlock social media's tremendous potential.

Indeed, the social media landscape is vast, complex, and overflowing with possibilities. It's essential, therefore, to equip yourself with the knowledge, understanding, and skills to navigate this vast expanse and use them to your advantage. As you traverse this expansive landscape, bear in mind the intricate balance of interaction and marketing you need to strike to fully leverage social media for your home-based business.

Embolden yourself. Immerse into the relentless rush of the social media streams. Forge your path. Make waves. And as you do, know that the social media landscape is not foreboding. It is, rather, an engaging and thrilling realm of limitless opportunities. As the subsequent chapters unfurl, you'll learn how to grab these opportunities and use them as your stepping stones to success.

Chapter 3. Leveraging the Key Social Media Platforms

In the expansive digital landscape, certain platforms have carved a niche for themselves, garnering a massive user base and transforming the way we communicate, share experiences, and most importantly, conduct business. If you're serious about catapulting your home-based enterprise to new heights, embracing and leveraging these platforms is no longer optional—it is essential.

3.1. The Big Four: Facebook, Instagram, LinkedIn and Twitter

Arguably the most influential social media platforms today are Facebook, Instagram, LinkedIn, and Twitter. Each possesses unique characteristics, catering to different demographics and supporting distinct content formats. Streamlining your presence on these platforms is the first step towards leveraging the full potential of social media for your business.

Facebook, with its root firmly planted in the very soil of today's digital ecosystem, has matured from a simple 'friend-connection' application to a gigantic marketing toolbox. Facebook Pages and Groups facilitate business promotion, while the Marketplace feature opens up a sea of opportunities for e-commerce ventures.

Instagram, owned by Facebook, has carved out its niche as a visually-driven platform. Capitalizing on user-generated content, influencer partnerships, and advertising options like Shoppable Posts, Instagram constitutes a sales-generating powerhouse for a gamut of businesses.

LinkedIn, on the other hand, is geared towards professionals and B2B interactions, making it an apt platform for establishing your brand as an industry thought-leader. Its advanced features like LinkedIn Articles and Slideshare presentations can be potently used for this objective.

Twitter's real-time news and conversation orientation make it a potent tool for amplifying brand visibility and engaging in direct conversations with consumers, prospects, and industry influencers.

3.2. Harnessing the Power of YouTube and Pinterest

As social media users' appetite for video content continues to increase, YouTube, the world's second largest search engine, comes into play. With the right YouTube strategy, including Search Engine Optimized (SEO) video content and well-organized playlists, you can effectively reach your audience and drive brand awareness.

Pinterest, with its unique 'pinning' feature of visual bookmarks, makes it a perfect platform for businesses dealing in home decor, fashion, food, and other visually appealing products. By leveraging its strong female-oriented user base and creating attractive pinboards, advertising on Pinterest can significantly enhance your brand visibility.

3.3. Utilizing Niche Networks

Niche social platforms like TikTok, Snapchat, and Reddit present a delightful opportunity to connect with hyper-specific audiences. With creative short-form video content, TikTok and Snapchat can particularly bolster brand visibility among younger demographics. Meanwhile, Reddit's discussion-based format allows for in-depth conversations with users interested in very specific topics, making it an ideal platform for niche marketing.

3.4. Hacks to maximize platform potency

Understanding the nuances of each social media platform is critical in creating platform-specific strategies in tune with their inherent strengths. Here are some universal hacks to enhance your performance:

1. **Understand your Target Audience**: Knowing who your prospective customers are, their preferences, and their social media behaviors can ensure your efforts resonate with them genuinely.

2. **Build a Strong Brand Persona**: Consistently represent your brand across platforms, using identifiable logos, a consistent tone of voice, and aligned messaging.

3. **High-quality Content**: Content is the king in social media. Create engaging, relevant, relatable, and high-quality content tailored per specific platform conventions.

4. **Use Analytics**: Use built-in analytics tools to measure and evaluate performance, iteratively improving your strategies through insights gained.

5. **Engage**, **Engage**, and **Engage**: Social media is all about interaction. Responding to comments, addressing feedback, joining relevant conversations all contribute to the strengthening of your brand's online community and its credibility.

By employing a strategic approach to select social media platforms, understanding their unique attributes, and aligning your business's social media strategies with the platforms' core strengths, your home-based business can experience a transformative growth, solidifying its place in the challenging digital world.

Chapter 4. Fundamentals of Social Media Marketing

Fundamentally, social media marketing is a facet of online marketing that utilizes diverse social media platforms to connect with the audience to build a brand, drive website traffic, and increase sales. It primarily revolves around creating and sharing content on social media networks to meet your marketing and branding objectives. Activity comprises posting text and image updates, videos, and other content to engage the audience, supplemented with paid social media advertising.

4.1. Understanding the Essence of Social Media Marketing

Social media marketing is a potent tool in the modern digital age, providing an avenue to establish direct links with your customers. By volunteering content that the audience finds valuable, you build strong and organic relationships, allowing for a steady conversion of potential customers into loyal fans and patrons of your business. The beauty of social media marketing lies in its approachability and inclusivity, irrespective of the size or nature of your venture. It can curtail marketing costs significantly while ensuring a wider reach targeted towards a desired customer base.

However, the very strength of social media also presents its challenge. The social media landscape is a whirlpool of content, with millions of businesses grappling for customer attention. The sheer volume can often be intimidating for home-based businesses. But don't worry. With the right strategies, it's not just manageable but also immensely rewarding.

4.2. Building a Goal-Oriented Strategy

The backbone of successful social media marketing is an infallible strategy. And the bedrock of this strategy is establishing clear and measurable marketing goals. The primary attempt should be to align these goals with your broader business strategy needs. As you set goals, attach each to corresponding metrics, or 'Key Performance Indicators' (KPIs), to measure progress effectively.

Take note:

- Aim for quality over quantity: A focused clientele who interacts and shares your content is more valuable than thousands with scanty interaction.

- Content is king: It has the power to attract, inspire, and convert potential clients.

- Patience pays: Success doesn't happen overnight; it requires consistent investment of time and resources.

- The competition is a source of inspiration: Keep an eye on your competitors; they can offer valuable data for keyword research and other insights.

4.3. Choosing the Right Platforms

Your choice of social media platforms is crucial in determining the success of your social media marketing. Not all social media platforms serve the same demographic or promote the same type of content. Understanding the demographic distribution across different platforms can help you choose the ideal platform to reach your target audience.

Keep these guidelines in mind:

- Facebook is versatile with a broad demographic, suitable for any business.

- Instagram appeals more to young adults and is excellent for businesses that rely heavily on images such as fashion, photography, and food.

- Twitter is great for businesses that want to keep their audience informed about updates.

- LinkedIn is ideal for B2B business and employment-oriented content.

- Pinterest could be a hit if your target audience is primarily women and your content is graphic-heavy.

4.4. Creating and Curating Engaging Content

In social media marketing, engaging content is king. The foremost consideration while creating or curating content should be the value it offers to your audience. Your content needs to talk to them, address their issues, and provide solutions. Here, the storytelling element of social media can be leveraged. Narrate your brand's journey, its values, and how it can make the customer's life better.

Ascertain the following:

- Keep content relevant and relatable.

- Focus on visual content—images, infographics, videos.

- User-generated content can boost engagement, building a community around your brand.

- Consistency is key to establishing your brand's voice and personality.

4.5. Mastering the Art of Social Listening and Engagement

This aspect, often neglected, is vital to your two-way communication with customers. Social listening refers to monitoring social media channels for any mentions of your brand, competitors, product, and more. It gives you insights into what's important to your audience. Engage by participating in discussions and social media communities, respond to comments, and provide customer support from within the platform. This can help turn the valuable insights into action strategies.

4.6. The Directive of Paid Social Advertising

While unpaid social content could build a slow and steady following, paid social media campaigns offer quick and assured results. It includes sponsored content and ads shown to users based on their interests, behavior, demographics, and more. Each social media platform provides different options for running ad campaigns, so understanding each is crucial for optimizing returns on your investment.

Successful social media marketing is all about maintaining a balance. A thumb rule could be the rule of thirds:

- 1/3 of your content promotes your brand or generates leads.
- 1/3 of your content shares ideas or stories from leaders in your industry or like-minded businesses.
- 1/3 of your content is based on personal interactions that help humanize your brand.

Armed with these fundamental social media marketing strategies, you can get started on your journey to grow your home-based business like never before. Remember, it's about conversations, community, connecting, and building relationships with transparency and trust. In this digitally connected era, marketing is all about nurturing relationships, and that's where social media marketing steps in. It's your time to shine in the social media spotlight.

Chapter 5. Building Your Brand Identity on Social Media

The exploration of building your brand identity on social media is a journey that starts by recognizing and understanding the key pillars of your brand and how they can be expressed uniquely through social media. Defining your brand on these platforms not only extends your reach but also presents opportunities to engage with your consumer base, build loyalty, and drive traffic towards your products and services.

5.1. Defining Your Brand

Your brand is the face of your business; it is your business's personality and the feelings it instills in others. It includes the visual elements like your logo, color palette, typography and imagery, but also extends to the more abstract elements like your mission, values, and the promise you make to your customers.

Getting very clear on what comprises your brand will help you ensure consistency across all social media platforms. Consistency is key in presenting a unified and easily recognizable image to your audience. This crystal-clear clarity will guide your decision-making and strategy in all aspects of social media presence, whether it's the content you post, the way you interact with followers, or how you deal with feedback and criticism.

5.2. Incorporating Your Brand Into Your Social Media Strategy

Now that you have defined your brand, the next step is to incorporate your brand into your social media strategy. This entails strategically using brand visual elements, messages, and voice in your social media profile descriptions, posts, and responses to comments.

With careful planning, your brand can be seamlessly integrated into all your social media touchpoints, creating a more engaging and immersive experience for your audience. An unmistakable brand voice can set you apart and foster recognition; bespoke brand aesthetics can appeal to the visual sensibilities of your audience; and compelling brand messages can engage and stir emotions.

The cardinal rule is consistency. Regular features that mirror your brand identity, hashtags associated with your brand, a steady posting schedule – everything contributes to strengthening your brand identity on social media.

5.3. Building Brand Recognition

The prominence of social media provides opportunities to build brand recognition. Brand recognition goes beyond simple awareness; it is about ensuring your brand stands out and is easily identifiable among a sea of competitors.

Think of it as a mosaic where all the little pieces – the color and design of your logo, the light and shade of your chosen palette, the tone of your communication, the aesthetic consistency across your posts – come together to create an indelible impression in the audience's mind.

Regular and consistent posting, establishing visual coherence, creating shareable branded content, using crafted hashtags, all are ways to build brand recognition. Moreover, engaging with your audience also has a significant role to play. This includes responding to comments, liking, and sharing user-generated content, and rewarding brand advocates, which can stimulate further interaction and enhance brand recognition.

5.4. Managing Your Brand Reputation

Brand reputation is an incredibly vital piece of the puzzle. The digital landscape of social media means that word of mouth now travels exceptionally fast, and managing a brand's reputation has become increasingly important.

Transparent communication, immediate response to potential crises, addressing customer complaints quickly, empathetically, and effectively, are all fundamental to managing your brand reputation on social media. Creating a plan in advance for potential crises, including who will respond, how, and what steps will be taken, can prevent a disastrous meltdown.

Moreover, encouraging positive reviews, rewarding customer advocacy, and proactively managing your online presence can lead to a solid brand reputation. Remember, consistency is the golden thread running through the entire social media fabric that holds it all together, fostering trust, and making your home-based business a success.

With these strategies, plans, and practical insights at your disposal, you can start confidently crafting your brand identity on social media. This might seem overwhelming to begin with, but by taking one step at a time and focusing on consistency, you will create a strong foundation for your home business on social media, making it a recognizable brand that is trusted by its audience.

Chapter 6. Creating Engaging Content for Your Audience

Creating engaging content for your audience is integral to any successful social media strategy. Indeed, effective online interaction often hinges more on the quality of content than the quantity. High-quality, engaging content will not only attract new followers to your platforms but will also keep your existing followers interested and active. This chapter provides a thorough, comprehensive, and long-winded exposition of how to best create engaging content tailored to your specific audience.

6.1. Defining Engaging Content

Engaging content is the linchpin to social media success. The term encompasses any content- be it tweets, posts, blogs, podcasts, infographics, videos, or webinars- that prompts your audience to interact with you. By interaction, we refer to activities such as likes, comments, shares, follow, re-tweets, or clicks on the link provided. Essentially, the more your audience interacts with your content, the more engaging it is.

So, how do you go about creating such engaging content? It's imperative to understand who your audience is, what they prefer, and what kind of content caters best to their preferences. This requires diligent research, rigorous data analysis, and a keen understanding of your target demographic.

6.2. Understanding Your Audience

Creating content without understanding your audience is akin to shooting arrows in the dark. It's essential to know who your audience is, what they like, their challenges, their online behavior, and their preferences.

Tools such as Google Analytics, Facebook Insights, or Twitter Analytics can offer invaluable insights into your audience demographics, behavior patterns, and content preferences. These tools allow you to identify key audience metrics such as age, gender, location, browsing habits, and even their preferred time for online activities.

Alternatively, conducting surveys or questionnaires can provide you with more personalized insights. These can assist in channelling your content creation efforts more accurately.

6.3. Types of Engaging Content and Their Applications

Equipped with an understanding of your audience, the next step is to ensure that the type of content you produce will resonate with them.

1. **Informative Content**: This includes blogs, articles, white papers, e-books, or posts that educate the audience about a particular subject relevant to your business. The idea here is to provide value to your audience, thereby establishing authority in your niche.

2. **Interactive Content**: Quizzes, polls, contests, giveaways, or live videos provoke audience interaction. This type of content allows the audience to participate actively, making them feel more involved.

3. **User-generated Content**: Encouraging users to share their experiences, reviews, testimonials, pictures, or videos not only leads to content generation but also fosters a sense of community and trust.

4. **Visual Content**: Infographics, memes, GIFs, videos, or images are visually engaging and often more shareable. They offer an

excellent avenue for encapsulating and presenting complex information in an easily digestible manner.

5. **Storytelling Content**: People relate to stories, and using this to your advantage can lead to higher engagement. You can share stories about your company, customer experiences, or even case studies.

Be sure to use the type of content that best suits your specific audience and business goals.

6.4. Harnessing the Power of Scheduling and Consistency

Despite having created engaging content, sharing it sporadically on your platforms may limit its potential reach. Consistency and scheduling are significant factors in ensuring that your content is seen by as many of your followers as possible. Tools like Hootsuite, Buffer, or Sprout Social can assist you in organizing and scheduling your content in advance. Regular consistent posts help maintain an active online presence, thus boosting audience engagement.

Remember, creating good content involves understanding your audience, selecting the appropriate type of content, leveraging the right tools, and promoting it consistently. By following these strategies, you'll be on your way to building a robust and engaging online presence for your home-based business. It's time to let your unique content connect, engage, and inspire your audience. Happy content creation!

Chapter 7. Mastering Social Media Advertising

Today's digital landscape is teeming with multiple platforms, technologies, and strategies to leverage. One such increasingly promising avenue is social media advertising. With the right knowledge, resources, and ambition, you can turn the complex channels of social media into a veritable powerhouse, capable of delivering stellar growth for your home-based business. This 'adventure guide' will illuminate your path, helping you to master the fundamentals, acquaint yourself with the key platforms, and develop a robust strategy for social media advertising.

7.1. Navigating the Landscape

To begin with, one must navigate the vast digital topography of social media platforms. Each channel offers a unique blend of audience demographics, characteristics, and advertising capabilities. To optimize the benefits reaped from social media advertising, it's essential not just to understand how each platform functions, but also to identify which will serve your business objectives most appropriately.

Facebook and Instagram, owned by the same parent company and sharing an ad platform, are two powerhouses of social media advertising. They offer extensive demographic targeting options and a variety of ad formats, such as static image, video, Carousel, and Collection ads. Instagram is especially effective for businesses with visually engaging content.

Twitter, on the other hand, is particularly suited for real-time engagement and conversation. Its advertising capabilities include Promoted Tweets, Promoted Accounts, and Promoted Trends, excellent avenues for expanding business and brand reach.

LinkedIn is another platform to consider, especially for B2B businesses, due to its professional demographic. Linkedin advertising offers Sponsored Content, Message Ads, Text Ads, and Dynamic Ads—each designed to tap into a different aspect of user behavioral patterns.

Then there's Pinterest, YouTube, Snapchat, and TikTok, each platform providing unique advertising opportunities that may be the perfect road to growth for some businesses, depending upon the demographics and content unique to each.

7.2. Formulating a Robust Advertising Strategy

Having navigated the landscape, the next step is to develop a robust and comprehensive social media advertising strategy. It should be rooted in your business goals, deeply understanding your target audience, choice of platforms, content curation, budget allocation, and performance tracking.

Start by identifying what you aim to achieve through your social media advertisements. Are you trying to drive website traffic, increase product sales, improve brand awareness, or something else? Even the most intricate and aesthetically pleasing advertisements can fall flat without a defined objective driving them.

Next is understanding and identifying your target audience. This involves not just demographic data like age, gender, and location, but also psychographic considerations such as attitudes, interests, and motivational factors.

Following this, consider which platform(s) would be most beneficial to use based on your target audience and marketing goals. Content curation is vital too – focus on creating engaging, relevant content while keeping it aligned with your brand and message.

Determining an optimal budget is another essential factor. It all depends on your business size, goals, and the specific platform. For instance, Facebook provides options like daily budget and lifetime budget, ensuring flexibility for every kind of advertiser.

Last but not least, tracking the performance of your campaigns will allow you to understand what's working and what needs adjustment. Analytics will provide insights into metrics like reach, engagement, conversion, and help you make informed decisions about your ongoing and future strategies.

7.3. Understanding Advertising Metrics and Analytics

Utilizing metrics to gauge the success of your advertising strategy is a crucial skill in the world of social media marketing. Knowing which precise metrics to monitor can spell the difference between an efficient campaign and one that wastes resources without achieving results.

Broadly speaking, the metrics can be divided into three categories. 'Awareness' metrics, which measure the size of your audience, 'Engagement' metrics, which evaluate interaction levels between your business and audience, and 'Conversion' metrics, which assess how effectively your ads are driving desired customer actions.

In 'Awareness' metrics, we look at impressions (the number of times your ad was displayed), reach (the number of people who saw your ad), and frequency (average number of times a person saw your ad).

'Engagement' metrics include likes, shares, comments, video views or clicks, which paint a broader picture of how your audience interacts with your content.

Last, 'Conversion' metrics delve into the number of actions taken, like making purchases, signing up for newsletters, or downloading an app. Conversion rate, click-through rate, and cost per action are key indicators here.

7.4. Implementing A/B Testing

Advertising is not just an art, it's a science. As such, the scientific method of hypothesize, test, evaluate, and learn is highly applicable. A/B testing, also known as split testing, is one such method used to compare two versions of an ad to discover which performs better.

A/B testing allows you to tweak every element of your ad: the image, the headline, the call to action, even the color scheme. By consistently running these tests, you can gather data to refine and optimize your ads constantly. It's a way to ensure that you are making the most of your advertising budget, investing in what truly works and discarding what doesn't.

Through the comprehensive understanding of social media advertising landscape, an intelligent advertising strategy formulation, diligent metrics monitoring and analytics utilization, and smart implementation of A/B testing, mastering social media advertising is within your grasp. It may seem daunting initially, with its technicalities and demands. But with time, patience, persistence, and the right brand of passion, you will see your home-based business skyrocket towards greater heights of success enabled by the power of effective social media advertising.

Chapter 8. Boost Your Business with Social Media Analytics

Being a sophisticated entrepreneur of the digital age, you understand the value of leveraging key social media platforms to foster your home-based business. However, with an overwhelming surge of data derived from various sources, managing and making sense of this data can pose a formidable challenge. This is where the gripping power of social media analytics steps in, providing essential insights and creating an informational backbone for strategic business decisions.

8.1. Entering the World of Social Media Analytics

Social media analytics is the process of gathering and analysing data from social networks such as Facebook, Instagram, Twitter, and LinkedIn, and then using that data to make informed business decisions. By tapping into social media analytics, you can authentically engage with your audience, optimise your content and ad strategy, thereby boosting your online presence and soon, your revenues.

It allows an array of benefits such as understanding the sentiments attached to your brand, knowing who your audience is, what content they engage with the most, and which platform brings more traction. This data then can be used to form strategies that appeal to your audience, continue producing engaging content, focus on platforms that bring more engagement and eventually, conversions.

8.2. Types of Social Media Analytics

Typically, social media analytics is divided into four broad categories: Descriptive Analytics, Diagnostic Analytics, Predictive Analytics, and Prescriptive Analytics.

1. Descriptive Analytics: This type provides an aggregate view of your historical data, giving you a holistic view of 'What happened?' It includes metrics like reach, impressions, engagement, and share of voice.

2. Diagnostic Analytics: This digs deeper into your data to understand 'Why did it happen?' It involves looking for patterns, trends and correlations. For example, you might find that posts with images get more engagement than text-only posts.

3. Predictive Analytics: This focuses on 'What will happen?' It uses statistical models and forecasts to predict future performance based on historical data.

4. Prescriptive Analytics: This provides actionable recommendations based on the analysis of 'What should we do?' It could suggest the best times to post or which type of content resonates most with your audience.

8.3. How to Garner Insights through Social Media Analytics

Getting started with social media analytics isn't as daunting as it seems. Follow this systematic approach.

1. Define Goals: Start by setting clear, measurable goals. What do you want to achieve with your social media strategy? Are you hoping to increase brand awareness, generate sales, or foster loyalty?

2. Identify Key Metrics: Depending on your goals, choose relevant

metrics or Key Performance Indicators (KPIs). These might include metrics around reach, engagement, conversions, and customer satisfaction.

3. Choose Analysis Tools: There are a plethora of social media analytics tools available in the market, choose one that best fits your needs. These range from built-in analytics offered by platforms like Facebook Insights and Twitter Analytics, to premium tools like Hootsuite and Buffer.

4. Analyze and Interpret: After accessing the data using chosen tools, analyze the patterns, trends, and insights. What does the data tell you? Are certain types of posts more successful? Is your audience more active at particular times?

5. Implement changes: Armed with these insights, make necessary adjustments to your social media strategy. This could involve producing different types of content, shifting focus to other platforms, or revising your posting schedule.

6. Measure and Adjust: The final step is to continually measure your performance against the set KPIs, and tweak your strategy as per insights gained.

8.4. Case Study: Leveraging Social Media Analytics for Growth

As an illustration of the potential of social media analytics, consider the case of a fledgling home-based entrepreneur who started selling handmade organic skincare products. Initially, her primary marketing approach was through word-of-mouth and distributing samples in her local community. She had created profiles on various social media platforms but lacked a targeted strategy.

She then decided to use social media analytics and started tracking her audience's preferences, the type of content that got maximum engagement, peak activity times, and sentiment around her products.

Using these insights, she curated targeted content, hosted live interaction sessions during peak activity periods, and addressed queries and concerns promptly, which directly boosted customer satisfaction.

In six months, her followers had tripled; engagement was four times higher, and her revenue shot up by 70%. Simply through implementing a structured approach backed by social media analytics, she was able to significantly grow her home-based business.

8.5. Conclusion

In a nut-shell, social media analytics is the secret weapon you need to outpace competition and heighten your home-business success. It is not just about stacking pieces of data, but about creating a meaningful dialogue with your customers, understanding them, and ultimately servicing them better. Even the subtlest of trends and patterns can have significant implications for your business.

Remember, in the fast-paced and dynamic world of social media, what worked yesterday might not work tomorrow. Hence, it is crucial to keep a continual eye on your analytics, understand the emerging trends, and adapt quickly. This will not only prognosticate your growth journey but also ensure you are riding the social media wave right.

As your digital bootstrapping foregoes ahead, don't forget that each number or statistic generated in your social media analytics, is a pulse of your digital audience. It is these heartbeats that will guide your journey to uncharted territories of business success. As you embark on this engrossing journey of translating data into growth, remember, even the sky isn't the limit!

Chapter 9. Cracking the Code: Social Media SEO

Social media SEO, or search engine optimization, is a crucial tool in enhancing the visibility of your home-based business online. It pertains to the organic strategies used to increase the visibility of content in social media searches, suggestions, and streams. Combining the power of SEO with social media strategies could be the game-changer your home-based business needs to climb the ranks in search engine result pages (SERPs) and get that much-desired traffic.

Before diving into the nitty-gritty details, it's critical to understand the beauty that underlies the synergy of SEO and social media. While SEO focuses on optimizing web content to surge in search results, social media aims to promote this content, encouraging engagement and increasing the visibility among a broad audience. This symbiotic relationship holds the potential for your home-based businesses to explode in growth and profitability.

9.1. The Basics: SEO for Social Media

The SEO used for social media is not much different from the techniques used for traditional websites. It utilizes keywords, quality of content, and engagement to ensure a better ranking on social media platforms.

1. **Keywords** - Regardless of the platform you are on, keywords play an essential role in SEO. Consider them as the gateways connecting your content with your target audience. Properly optimizing your posts with relevant keywords increases the chance of being discovered by potential customers. Depending on the social media platforms, keywords can be used in different ways.

2. **Quality of content** - While keywords help you connect with your audience, the quality of content ensures they stay connected. Consistently delivering quality content establishes trust with the audience, encouraging them to interact with your business more and more.

3. **Engagement** - Lastly, social media thrives on engagement. The more likes, comments, and shares your posts have, the more likely it is to appear in the feeds of others, thereby increasing your visibility.

9.2. Mastering Keyword Optimization on Different Platforms

Operating on different social media platforms means dealing with different user interfaces. Consequently, the approach to SEO varies as well.

1. **Facebook** - Small tricks like including keywords in the 'About' section or using the 'Story' section to incorporate keywords can significantly improve your visibility on Facebook. Regularly use your target keywords in your posts. However, avoid infringement into keyword-stuffing territory.

2. **Twitter** - Utilize hashtags for keyword optimization on Twitter. Hashtags work like keywords and help Twitter users discover content related to specific topics. Ensure your tweet character count is conserved by keeping them concise yet impactful.

3. **Instagram** - Here, keywords can be used in the username, account name, or the description. However, the prominent use is in hashtags. It's advisable to use a mix of popular and niche hashtags for better visibility of your posts.

4. **LinkedIn** - SEO is best served in the 'About' section, job

description, and expertise. Relevant keywords used professionally are more likely to attract their intended audience.

5. **Pinterest** - For Pinterest, incorporate keywords in the pin descriptions, board names, and even in your business name in order to improve visibility.

9.3. Creating High-Quality, Shareable Content

SEO and social media both thrive on unique, high-quality content. Creating shareable content will trigger the audience to share it, creating backlinks, which significantly boosts your SEO. Always ensure your content is relevant, relatable, creative, and genuine.

9.4. Encouraging Engagement and User Interaction

Impressions are great, but interaction is the key to the kingdom on social media. The higher your engagement rate, the more visible your pages become. Think about sparking conversations, asking for opinions, or running surveys and contests. Highlight positive interactions to incentivize future engagements.

9.5. Utilizing Social Media Analytics

Be proactive in understanding what works for you using social media analytics. These tools provide insights about the reach of your posts, the degree of interaction, the demographics of your audience, and much more. Use this information to tailor your SEO strategies effectively.

In all, remember that SEO is a marathon, not a sprint. It might take some time before you can see the results. However, with consistent effort and mindful strategies, the benefits are enormous and long-lasting. Remember that your ultimate goal should always be value delivery and building authentic relationships with your audience. This will not only enhance your visibility in the world of social media but also pave the way for sustainable growth of your home-based business.

Chapter 10. Crisis Management on Social Media

The digital age, especially with the surge in social media platforms, has opened a Pandora's Box of opportunities. But it is also true that it has thrown open a murky minefield crisscrossed with moments of crises. In the twinkling of an eye, a minor issue can spiral into a massive crisis, capable of tarnishing an otherwise stellar reputation. Respect and reputation, built over years, can be shattered in moments. In these times of reputation crisis, well planned, systematic measures can save the day. This chapter focuses on effective crisis management procedures in the vulnerable world of social media.

10.1. Recognizing a Crisis on Social Media

First, it's vital to recognize a crisis when it shows up. A crisis could take various forms - a scandal in the company, a faulty delivery, or a rampaging tweet storm condemning your product or service. It is essential to stay vigilant, actively monitor social networks, and be aware of the murmurings and conversations about your business. Automated social listening tools can be very effective in alerting you of a potential crisis.

Essentially, your arsenal for crisis prediction should include having a good understanding of your brand sentiment analysis, and keeping tabs on rapidly changing thoughts about your products, services or ethics.

10.2. Preparation: Laying Out a Crisis Communication Strategy

A crisis is not the time to think, but to act. Preparation is half the battle won. Investing time and effort in developing a crisis communication strategy well in advance can act as a robust armour.

Key aspects of this strategy would include: . Identifying spectrum of possible crises for your home-based business. . Preparing a crisis communication team. . Allocating roles and responsibilities to each team member. . Establishing a predefined notification system to alert the crisis communication team. . Drafting preliminary responses for different potential crisis scenarios.

10.3. Responding to a Crisis with Transparency and Empathy

It's not just about responding, it's about responding properly. The critical principles governing any response are honesty, transparency, and empathy. Any attempt to cover up, defer responsibility, or remain silent can further aggravate the situation. It's crucial to own up, sincerely apologize, and assure your audience that steps are being taken to rectify the mistake.

10.4. Post-Crisis Management

After a crisis has been dealt with, do not presume everything's back to normal. Reflect on the crisis, the reaction to it, and most importantly, learn from it. This introspection will help in honing your crisis strategy and averting potential future crises.

10.5. Planning Ahead: Updating Your Crisis Communication Strategy

An event as significant as a social media crisis prompts a need to revisit and revise your crisis communication strategy. No plan is flawless and reflecting on these shortcomings can lead to a plan that is more robust and comprehensive. Your revised strategy should be tested with crisis drills or simulations that help ensure your business's resilience in real-life scenarios.

By strategically planning, diligently practicing, and tactfully maneuvering, you can master the unsettling torrents of a social media crisis. This crisis management strategy can safeguard your home-based business's reputation, protecting your brand, and paving the path towards future-proof growth in the dynamic landscape of social media.

Chapter 11. Looking Ahead: The Future of Social Media for Home-Based Businesses

As we round off this comprehensive deep-dive into the remarkable world of social media for home-based businesses, the question that naturally arises in your mind, the forward-looking entrepreneur, might be - 'what lies ahead in the landscape of social media?' Undoubtedly, extrapolating future trends from the present can be fraught with challenges, volatile as the digital realm is. Nevertheless, some key social media trends and shifts are discernible, shaping the future and offering a glimpse into the transformative course that awaits home-based businesses. Let's embark together on this forward-looking journey, exploring the exciting road ahead.

11.1. The Advent of Augmented Reality and Virtual Reality

Evolving technologies such as Augmented Reality (AR) and Virtual Reality (VR) are gearing up to revolutionize the way brands interact with their audience on social media. While AR adds digital elements to a live view, VR implies a fully immersive experience. These technologies could be exceptionally advantageous to home-based businesses, offering potential customers a unique, interactive, and engrossing virtual experience. For instance, with AR filters, you could allow customers to virtually 'try on' your products or visualize them in their space before purchase. Conversely, VR could provide an immersive brand experience, similar to a physical store, from the comfort of their home.

11.2. Social Shopping and Social Commerce Expansion

Social media platforms have begun to integrate e-commerce components into their functionalities, allowing users to shop directly from the social app. For instance, Instagram's 'Shoppable Posts' let users buy items they see and love directly within the app. This evolution of social commerce promises a streamlined consumer journey with improved conversion rates. As a home-based business, leveraging this trend would mean simplifying the shopping process for your customers and potentially boosting sales.

11.3. Personalization and AI-driven Content

Artificial Intelligence (AI) and machine learning technologies are increasingly being employed to personalize user experiences on social media. Platforms are using AI to analyze individual user behavior and predict the type of content that would be most appealing, leading to customized feeds and recommendations. This implies a much more target-oriented approach for your brand's marketing efforts relying heavily on AI-driven insights.

11.4. The Growing Scale of Influencer Marketing

Influencer marketing is envisaged to continue its ascendency, with more brands teaming up with influencers for product endorsements. Micro-influencers, with their niche followers, are particularly beneficial for home-based businesses. They can enhance brand visibility, build trust, and generate engagement more economically than celebrity influencers. As a home-based business, partnering with micro-influencers relevant to your industry could amplify your brand's reach and authenticity.

11.5. Rise of Short-Form Video Content and Live Streams

Video content has become a staple of social media, undergoing continued growth. Particularly, short-form videos and live streams are hugely popular, prominently driven by platforms like TikTok. Such engaging video content can increase visibility and boost audience interaction for your home-based business.

11.6. Focus on Privacy and User Data Protection

With enhanced scrutiny on data privacy, social media platforms are adopting more user-centric privacy policies. This shift could influence how you reach out to your audience, requiring more transparency and user consent for data-based marketing strategies.

11.7. Sustainability and Social Responsibility

Social users are gravitating towards brands that uphold social responsibility and sustainable practices. Thus, highlighting your business's dedication to ethical sourcing, sustainable packaging, or other socially responsible policies can help build a loyal, conscious customer base.

In summary, the future of social media for home-based businesses is loaded with transformative possibilities. While this might mean staying continually updated and adapting to new trends, the potential rewards in terms of business growth, brand visibility, and customer engagement are immense. And with this hopeful glance at the horizon, we conclude our social media expedition, leaving you to navigate your ship towards the sea of success. Embrace the change, pioneer the new, and watch your home-based business flourish in this dynamically evolving social media landscape.

www.ingramcontent.com/pod-product-compliance
Lightning Source LLC
La Vergne TN
LVHW010041070326
832903LV00071B/4687